CU00819262

Waymarking
public rights of way

Distributed by:
Countryside Agency Publications
PO Box 125
Wetherby
West Yorkshire LS23 7EP

Tel: 0870 120 6466
Fax: 0870 120 6467
Email: countryside@twoten.press.net
Minicom: 0870 120 7405
(for the hard of hearing)

103723172

CONTENTS

Illustrations based on those by Anne Roper in *Footpaths*, reproduced with kind permission of the BTCV.

Introduction

The term waymarking means marking objects along a public right of way. It complements signposting, which shows where a right of way leaves the metalled road and indicates its initial direction. Waymarking enables users to follow a path accurately and confidently at points where they might otherwise have difficulty.

Waymarking benefits not only users of rights of way but also farmers and landowners. It increases users' enjoyment of the countryside and prevents unintentional trespass.

Carrying out waymarking is a simple and very practical way in which a parish council, local group or individual landowner or occupier can help to look after the rights of way in their area. This booklet explains how to go about it.

The waymarking system

The recommended system in England (and Wales) uses small coloured arrows to show the direction of the path and also to act as a target when viewed from a distance. A different colour is used for each category of right of way:

- public rights of way that are footpaths are waymarked using yellow arrows;
- bridleways are waymarked with blue arrows;
- byways open to all traffic and other routes that may legally be used by wheeled vehicles are waymarked with red arrows, but they are intended only to show the status of the route and not to indicate whether it is physically suitable for vehicles.

If the status of a path changes along its length, so does the colour of the waymarking arrows. Where a right of way is part of a special route, such as a National Trail or circular walk, the arrows are used in conjunction with the route's own symbol.

Planning a waymarking scheme

Once the waymarks are in place, many people will rely on them and will expect to be able to follow the route without the help of a map or guidebook. Therefore, waymarks should not be placed at random, but must be part of an overall scheme.

Initially it may not be practical or possible to waymark all of the paths in an area, so it is useful to bear in mind that the majority of walkers look for attractive circular walks of about two to five miles in length, which they can follow and enjoy with confidence. Those who are riding or cycling will typically cover around 10 to 15 miles.

Start by linking through routes, for example from one surfaced road to the next or from village to village. Try to include paths with the finest views, those that pass places of interest and any where users can park a car or unload a horse-box. Build this up into a network of waymarked routes that offer an attractive variety of walking or riding opportunities.

Although waymarking is an ideal way of increasing users' choice by indicating little-known or recently restored paths, you should avoid inviting people to follow paths where you know they will encounter serious problems. Paths that are impossibly overgrown, badly eroded or obstructed should not be waymarked until these problems have been resolved by the highway authority.

Working with the highway authority

It is essential to contact the highway authority at an early stage, and to follow its advice and instructions. The highway authority is the county, unitary or metropolitan authority or London borough for the area.

A highway authority is responsible for the rights of way in its area. Its duties include erecting and maintaining signposts wherever a footpath, bridleway or byway leaves a surfaced road, and waymarking those rights of way where, in the authority's opinion, it is necessary to help anyone unfamiliar with the locality to follow the route.

The highway authority will be able to help in a number of ways. In planning the scheme, it will:

- help to check the definitive map (the legal record of rights of way in the area) to confirm the correct line of each path;
- know about any recent changes, such as paths that have been diverted;
- know about any disputed paths in the area and give advice on these or other difficulties;
- assist or give advice in any negotiations with landowners or farmers.

For the practical work, most authorities can supply free waymarking signs and many can provide paint in the correct colours and other materials. The authority might be able to arrange for other work to be carried out at the same time to make the waymarking as effective as possible, such as erecting any signposts that are needed where paths leave the metalled road, and minor path clearance.

It is often possible for an authority to extend its insurance cover to indemnify volunteers while they are carrying out work on the authority's behalf.

Working with landowners, occupiers and the parish council

It is important to contact all of the landowners and occupiers of the land crossed by the paths in the scheme. The law requires that they be consulted, and their consent is needed (preferably in writing) before waymarks can be placed on anything that is the owner's or occupier's property, such as a fence post or part of a stile.

Most owners and occupiers are aware of the benefits and will readily agree to their paths being waymarked. Try to arrange to walk the paths with them to agree the best location for each waymark. It is useful at this stage to obtain permission to replace or repaint waymarks as necessary.

The occupier or owner may also offer to help in practical ways, even to the extent of supplying the waymarks themselves. For example, the Country Business and Landowners' Association has packs of waymarks that it sells to its members. If any difficulties or disputes do arise, you should refer back to the highway authority for further advice.

If the parish council is not already involved, it should be contacted. It may have a member who is particularly interested in rights of way and who is able to assist in approaching the landowners and occupiers or finding out who they are.

Problem paths

There will normally be no difficulty in finding out from the highway authority which rights exist over each of the paths in the scheme and, therefore, what colour waymarks to use. However, rights of way that are still shown on the definitive map as 'roads used as public paths' (RUPPs) can be a problem.

All RUPPs are due to be reclassified to Restricted Byways once the appropriate section of the Countryside and Rights of Way Act commences (expected to be in 2002). In the meantime, RUPPs can be waymarked using the colour that corresponds to the rights that the authority currently believes exist over the particular route. This will usually be red for byway rights or blue for a bridleway. If the status of the route is subsequently found to be different, then the waymarks will need to be changed.

Occasionally, difficulties can arise on other paths, either because the path is not yet recorded on the definitive map or because someone (a path user or the farmer or landowner) believes that the status shown on the definitive map is incorrect. Follow the highway authority's advice and be prepared to change the waymarks, if necessary, once these difficulties have been resolved.

It is important to appreciate that waymarking a path cannot take away any 'higher' rights that may exist. For example, the fact that a path is shown on the definitive map as a bridleway and is waymarked in blue does not invalidate any higher (unrecorded) vehicular rights that might exist over the route.

Permissive paths

Permissive paths are paths that are not public rights of way, but which the landowner has agreed can be used by the public, with certain conditions.

The highway authority's duties do not include waymarking permissive paths. Even so, where such an agreement has been made it may be sensible for the route to be included in the waymarking scheme. Ask the authority for advice on the arrows to be used. Some authorities use standard colours corresponding to the type of use that has been agreed, eg yellow arrows on a path that can be used only by walkers. Others prefer a non-standard colour, such as white, to emphasise that the path is not a public right of way. In either case, simple notices should be put up at each end of the path explaining that it is permissive and listing the conditions under which it can be used.

Waymarking in upland areas

Special thought should be given before waymarking paths over mountains or remote moorland. These are places where inexperienced walkers or riders can easily get lost, but the widespread use of waymarking posts will be out of keeping in such areas. Waymarks can also encourage a false sense of security, putting users in danger should the weather suddenly deteriorate. Information may need to be given, particularly at the start of a route, about the hazards of going into these areas.

The practical work

Type of waymarks

Most waymarking is now carried out using printed plastic or metal signs fixed with galvanised nails. This is quick and easy, and ensures that the waymarking has a uniform appearance, although such waymarks can only be attached to wooden fences, stiles and gateposts. They must not be nailed to trees as this causes damage.

The traditional, and still the most versatile method is to paint the waymarking arrows. While this takes longer and can only be done in dry weather, painted arrows can be adapted to convey a special meaning and can be applied to a wider range of surfaces, including trees, stone and brick.

The arrow must be of the dimensions shown. It is easy to draw if based on a 90-mm diameter circle.

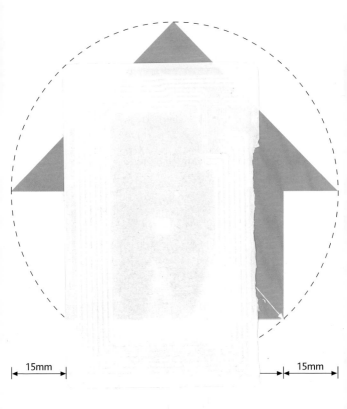

15mm

15mm

The correct waymarking colours are:

Footpaths
Yellow
BS 08 E 51
Munsell 3.75Y 8.5/12

Bridleways
Blue
BS 20 E 51
Munsell 5P P7/8

Byways open to all traffic
Red
BS 06 E 55 (approximate)
Munsell 10 R 5/14

Positioning

Waymarks are used in the same way as traffic signs, ie facing the oncoming walker or rider and with a different set of waymarks for each direction of travel. A '12 o'clock' arrow means the path goes straight ahead; a '3 o'clock' or '9 o'clock' arrow indicates a right-angle turning to the right or left, etc.

It is important that the angle of each arrow is as accurate as possible, even when the route is obvious on the ground,

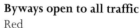

Straight on

as this will give confidence at the more difficult sites. To determine the angle, imagine the arrow as if it was flat on the ground. Temporarily fix or sketch the waymark in position then stand well back to check the angle as it will appear to approaching users. If possible, get at least one other person to confirm that the arrow conveys the proper direction.

The sites chosen should be as permanent and vandal resistant as possible. Stiles and gateposts are often suitable, although you should not put a waymark on the

Turn right

opening part of a gate. Bear in mind that a horserider's eye level will be higher than that of a walker; they may miss arrows that are not well above the ground.

The number of waymarks should be kept to the minimum necessary to make the route clear. Extra waymarks may be needed through a wood or other area with many alternative paths. They can be removed later or allowed to fade if the right of way becomes better defined. A turning from a major to a minor path may also need more than one arrow, or a larger arrow, if the walker's or rider's attention is to be attracted.

It is helpful to include an arrow at the start of the route where the path leaves the metalled road, so that users can see the path is waymarked and know which signs to follow.

Bear right

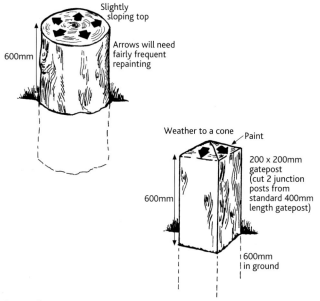

Peeled log: as large a diameter as possible

Slightly sloping top

Arrows will need fairly frequent repainting

600mm

Weather to a cone

Paint

200 x 200mm gatepost (cut 2 junction posts from standard 400mm length gatepost)

600mm

600mm in ground

Junctions

The best solution at a complicated junction is to ask the highway authority to supply a traditional fingerpost. This has the advantage of being easily recognised from a distance and conveying accurately the direction of each path. Other information such as destination and distance can be given, with the standard arrow included to give consistency. However, fingerposts are costly and prone to vandalism.

There are a number of other solutions, although each has some disadvantages. The most simple is to erect a special junction post with a series of waymarking arrows on each face, but this can look cluttered and confusing. Another suggestion is to use a large log, or half of a stout gatepost, sunk into the ground with arrows on the top. The weakness here is that the arrows will not be visible from a distance and will weather more quickly. Junction signs are occasionally made in the style of a small road sign, but they can be complicated to paint, especially if more than one colour is involved, and it may be difficult to find a suitable surface on which to put a sign.

Whichever solution is adopted, a confirmatory arrow on each path as it leads away from the junction will help to reinforce users' confidence.

Problem sites

Problems arise where the standard arrow cannot accurately convey which route should be taken, for example, which side of a wall or other field boundary the walker should follow. In these situations, the shaft of the arrow can be extended and curved through 45 or 90 degrees to give a clearer picture of the route.

In the examples below, illustrations (a) show how the standard arrow can mislead, and illustrations (b) show the use of the curved arrow.

The curved arrow should be used with care, and only in situations where the standard arrow is not suitable. The preferable solution is to ensure that the route is clear on the ground.

Where should the waymark be placed?

Wall

Path

a)

This arrow misleads: walkers take wrong side of wall

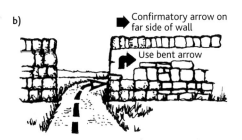

b)

Confirmatory arrow on far side of wall

Use bent arrow

Where standard waymarks are not suitable

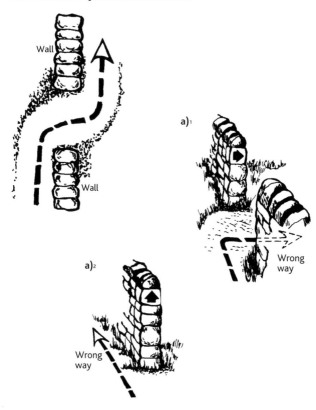

Wall

Wall

a)₁

Wrong
way

a)₂

Wrong
way

a)₃

Wrong
way

b) Correct route taken

Use bent arrow

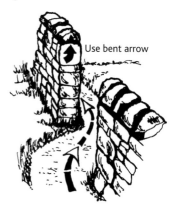

Large fields

When crossing a large field, particularly where the land rises in the middle to obscure the far boundary, the walker or rider has to set off with no target to aim for. The solution in cultivated fields is for the surface of the right of way to be reinstated after ploughing and for the line to be made apparent on the ground. Farmers are legally required to do this, and to ensure that the line through the growing crops remains apparent at all times.

A carefully angled arrow at the point of departure, and a clearly visible stile or gate once the next boundary comes in view, will help to keep the correct line in use. It is helpful to paint the top 0.2m of the stile or gate post in white to attract the eye, or to erect a tall target post topped with a white disc.

Erecting waymarking posts

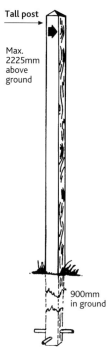

Tall post

Max. 2225mm above ground

900mm in ground

If it is necessary to erect posts for the waymarks, use at least 100 x 100mm hardwood, or softwood timber that has been pressure treated with preservative. Posts need to stand at least 0.75-1.0m above ground level but taller posts, up to 2.2m high, are useful in some situations as a marker or to stand above wayside vegetation. Try to chose a position where the post will not be used as a rubbing post by farm animals.

Fixing cross bars to the base helps to hold the post securely and to resist vandalism; use metal pipes pushed through drilled holes as shown in the drawing or short wooden bars nailed to two adjacent sides of the post.

To install a post, dig a hole to the correct depth, put the post in position, and replace the soil as firmly as possible by ramming down each 25mm layer with a suitable tool.

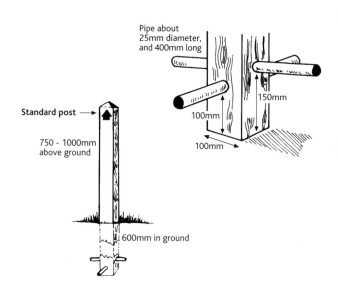

Pipe about 25mm diameter, and 400mm long

150mm

100mm

100mm

Standard post

750 - 1000mm above ground

600mm in ground

Equipment for waymarking

Tools

Useful tools for surface cleaning and minor clearance around a waymark include a wire brush, curved Surform, sickle, folding saw and bush pruners. A hammer and galvanised nails will be needed to install plastic or metal waymarks.

Paint

An oil-based undercoat, followed by a gloss topcoat, is the most lasting. Non-toxic paints must be used to ensure that there is no danger to livestock. Waymarking uses very little paint, so only small tins are needed, and paint can be decanted into a suitable container for use on site.

Brushes

Small brushes are required, with a fine flitch brush for the arrow corners. White spirit for cleaning should be taken in a suitable container, and a rag will also be useful.

Stencil

A stencil can be used either to paint directly over or to give an outline shape that can be marked with a pencil or fine point. Old vinyl flooring is pliable and easy to cut for this purpose. The centre piece can be used as a temporary waymark to help to choose the correct angle, or to mask over an arrow if a background colour is being painted to increase the arrow's visibility.

Looking after the waymarking

Once all of the waymarks are in place it is useful to arrange for someone who does not know the path to make sure the whole route can be followed accurately and without difficulty.

The waymarking should be checked every few months to make sure that all of the arrows are still in place and continue to convey the correct meaning. This is a good opportunity to look for early signs of other problems that might affect users' enjoyment of the route. Any such problems should be reported to the highway authority.

Occasionally waymarks may be stolen or vandalised, particularly those at the start of a path or close to built-up areas, and they should be replaced promptly. Beyond this, all that is necessary is to spruce up the scheme every few years by giving painted signs a fresh coat and replacing printed signs that have faded or become brittle.

Looked after in this way, your waymarking will help to ensure that the paths can be followed accurately and are enjoyable to use for many years.

Further advice

Details of all Countryside Agency publications are included in the **Countryside Agency Publications Catalogue** (CA2, free), available from:
Countryside Agency Publications,
PO Box 125, Wetherby,
West Yorkshire LS23 7EP.
Telephone: 0870 120 6466
Fax: 0870 120 6467
Email: countryside@twoten.press.net
Minicom: 0870 120 7405
(for the hard of hearing)

Publications may also be ordered from our on-line catalogue on the Agency's website: www.countryside.gov.uk

Useful publications

Footpaths: a practical conservation handbook, Elizabeth Agate, British Trust for Conservation Volunteers, 1996, £9.95. Gives detailed advice on all practical aspects of rights of way work, including further information on waymarking.

Out in the country: where you can go and what you can do (CA9), revised edition 2000, Free. The Agency's guide to the public's rights and responsibilities in the countryside.

A guide to definitive map procedures (CCP 285) revised edition 1996, Free. Outlines the procedures for changing the definitive map.

Rights of way: a guide to law and practice, John Riddall and John Trevelyan, Open Spaces Society and Ramblers' Association, third edition 2001. Price £20. Contains information on the principal legislation concerning access to the countryside, plus advice on practical path work.

Working with others

The work involved in planning and carrying out a waymarking scheme is easier if it is shared between a small group of people. Many groups of volunteers carry out not only waymarking, but also a wide range of other essential tasks such as clearing paths and building bridges and stiles. Highway authorities welcome and rely on their help in keeping rights of way open for everyone to enjoy.

The highway authority may be able to put you in touch with a group in your area, or you can write (enclosing a stamped, addressed envelope) to:

Ramblers' Association
1-5 Wandsworth Road
London SW8 2XX
Tel: 0207 339 8500
Fax: 0207 339 8501
Email: ramblers@london.ramblers.org.uk
www.ramblers.org.uk

British Trust for Conservation Volunteers
36 St Mary's Street, Wallingford
Oxon OX10 0EU
Tel: 01491 839766
Fax: 01491 839646
Email: information@btcv.org.uk
www.btcv.org.uk

British Horse Society
Stoneleigh Deer Park, Kenilworth
Warwicks CV8 2XZ
Tel: 01926 707700
Fax: 01926 707800
Email: enquiry@bhs.org.uk
www.bhs.org.uk

LARA (Motoring Organisations' Land Access and Recreation Association)
PO Box 20, Market Drayton
Shropshire TF9 1WR
Tel: 01630 657627
Fax: 01630 658928
Email: LARAHQ@aol.com
www.LARAGB.org